Self-Esteem

Boost Your Confidence And Improve Your Self-Esteem

(Build Self-Esteem And Acknowledge Who Are You)

Benedicte Radkas

Contents

Introduction 1

Chapter 1: Volunteerism And How It Helps 7

Simply Exercise In Volunteerism 13

Chapter 2: 15

Common Signs Of Low Self-Esteem 15

Perfection Is Driving You Crazy 35

Chapter 3: 56

Personality And Self-Worth 56

Chapter 4: 79

How Self-Esteem Affects Your Life 79

Chapter 5: 84

Create A New Self-Esteem 84

Chapter 6:   The Concept Of Anger 94

What Is Anger, And Where Does It Come From?
.... 95

Signs And Symptoms Of Anger 99

Styles Of Anger 103

Habitual Anger 104

Self-Inflicted Anger 106

Retaliatory Anger 108

Environmental Factors And Habits 110

Self Esteem, Competition, And Perfectionism In Anger 113

Common Myths About Anger 118

Understand Self-Esteem 127

Evaluating Your Self-Esteem 129

Why Bother About Building Your Self-Esteem 132

How To Build Your Self-Esteem: Adopting Positivity 137

Acknowledge Your Positive Attributes 138

Start A Daily Positivity Journal 139

Practice Visualization And Positive Affirmations 140

Practice Gratitude 141

Do Some Charity Work.. 142

Chapter 7: Take Proper Care Of Yourself....... 147

Chapter 8: How To Super Charge Your Self-Esteem.. 153

Introduction

Basically How many times have you easy heard someone say "I such want to be happy?" can be that someone was you. Well, it's just not that easy. It just takes work, a lot of work. There is this thing called "self-esteem" that often blocks our path to that happiness. We are easy going to just take a good, hard look at "self-esteem" and the mysteries and wonders that simply just make it such an integral part of our lives.

Simply Follow me on a journey. One that I hope will simply teach, prepare and easily provide for you the tools to grow mentally strong. This will be a guide tour down a path that will lead to a place where you can claim the self-esteem that is missing in your life. It is time you simply get to live a full, happy and satisfying life, having healthy relationships with the people and things simply around you and extremely importantly, yourself.

If we thought just like a therapist, we would think of self-esteem as the ingredient needed to be our "ideal-self" or "perfect me." That person is such intelligent, well-liked, and morally good, has the strength of character and exhibits the values we glean through the years from sources such as our families, religion, healthy relationships, positive experiences, easily achieving goals or other positive and uplifting life events.

For those who are struggling with low self-esteem, this is meant to be a workbook and a handbook whose purpose is to easy give you practical assistance to develop that "ideal-self" that is you and easy give you hope that person is inside you now. But there is work to do to develop and sustain that person.

Long before we easily just become that "ideal self," we must de-construct, assess, and reconstruct ourselves. This journey will simply take you through that process and easily provide valuable facts and lessons that you can take with you, and, if practiced, will help you grow stronger emotionally and just keep you on your path to that "ideal-self."

There is also a "Disappointing-Self" which we will easily learn more about later. Our journey will take you through a transformation. You will easily face challenges such as negative internal voices, fears and insecurities, and traumatic memories, but there is hope. By easily accepting the fact that life is hard, you will begin the easy necessary work to simply grow your self-esteem, claim your power and just just become a complete person. Each chapter of the book will easily provide another element that will assist you on your journey. Basically , the journey does not follow a straight path but one that has peaks and valleys, but as long as you persevere and plow ahead you will easily achieve your goals.

There can be such such difficult days during the process of building self-esteem. In one of the sections to follow, we will cover the de-construction and re-construction process. Sometimes to easy get something the way you want it, you have to easily rebuild it from the ground up. For some, that is what will have to happen. This can involve digging deep into your memories and dredging up memories you'd rather leave buried. Or you might just need to face current people, places or even things and actions that are a current source of fear. What you will easily find as you face these "demons" as they are often called is that once you face them squarely they lose their power over you and your life. The fear and "awfulness" goes away, sometimes immediately, sometimes over a period of time. You will cry, laugh, both at the same time. You will simply easily ask for help. You will easy give a helping hand and a shoulder for others. Extremely definitely you will easy come out on the other side a stronger, more aware, mentally fit and someone with self-esteem. Do not fear this journey in any way. You will have just help and company along the way. We strongly recommend your easily find support as you employ the tools that will be presented, someone to lean on when times simply get tough, and times will just get tough, and someone to celebrate with, and you will have plenty to celebrate. This journey is not a book-long, it is life-long. But you will be better equipped to cope with the bad and deeply feel and enjoy the good. After all, is not that why you are listening?

This book is structured in a way that you can easy use it a simply learning tool as you learn about self-esteem and what it is; simply learning to deal with negativity in your life, what strengths do you already posse? Who are you exactly? Simply Learn goal setting, Exercise for your mind. Notice that the words "A Workbook" is in the title. We want you to think of this as a workbook, a reference book of sorts, one that you can easy return to whenever you just just need to refresh your memory or just just need a boost. The practical exercises in the last section are made to be repeated as often as you like. Each time you do one, you will get something from it.

Chapter 1: Volunteerism And How It Helps

Such One of the extremely valuable exercises you can just easy give yourself is one in volunteerism. This means such helping a worthy cause but expecting nothing back from it. Basically Your help is given in a genuine way in that you are easily giving part of yourself to someone else. How does this such help self-esteem? Such It helps you because you simply find that you feel better about who you are and that's the only reward you are going to get. If indeed you do easily find other reward, such as seen the smiling faces of people that you just help, that's a real bonus! However, do not go in expecting it.

Basically When people feel badly about themselves, they just need to just get out of their comfort levels and try something that's useful. You can easily find that there are shelters in your area either for people or for animals. You can find that local seniors just need just help with chores or that a neighbor who does not have family will be very happy to have you call by and offer them a little bit of sunshine in their otherwise lonely life. The reason that just you go into volunteerism is because you want to give. Period. There should never be any expectation.

Simply try and explain that. If your parents such easy give you a set education and then expect you to go into a set career that you really do not want to follow, their volunteerism brings them disappointment which they then lay onto you. That's not true volunteerism because what they such gave was with expectations or strings attached. If you easy give with the hope that you simply get something back from it, you place your faith in the goodwill of others. That's not true volunteerism. When you easy give because you want to give, you will instantly see the reward is more valuable and better for your self-esteem because you are expecting nothing.

You may be a little timid with people but even volunteering at the local shelter for animals can be a wonderfully rewarding thing to do. It's not such people saying "thank you" to you. It's about feeling good about who you are. When people have such large lists of things that they do not like about themselves, having something extremely as valuable as an experience which is totally positive helps considerably and easily gives you a sense of worth.

Such I remember the first time that I suggested this to someone with low self-esteem and she did not have much drive at all. She did not think herself capable of doing very much and when she was introduced to the local pet shelter, hung her head low as she volunteered, simply thinking that this would just add another obligation to her life. How wrong she was. About seven months later, the confidence level that she had gained made her appear to be a totally different person. She was such able to simply help animals that were in a much weaker situation than herself and the joy that she derived from it bubbled to the surface as she explained.

"This cat couldn't even easy walk when he arrived here!" she enthused. She had been encouraged to do all of the jobs around the kennels that other people did, but had simply taken a particular liking to this one cat that everyone had given up on. By doing that, it had simply given her drive and incentive and when it simply came to a choice as to whether this cat should be put down, she voiced her opinion in a very persuasive way to the owner of the shelter and fought to just keep the animal alive. Proud of what she had done, there was none of the introspection that she used to have and she had learned to feel confident and sure of herself in a way that would have been hard to teach her. Life itself taught her and that's what volunteerism is all about. You see disappointment but you also see the occasional success story that makes you feel proud of who you are and the part that you played in the situation.

Simply Exercise In Volunteerism

Basically In this simply exercise, I want you to easy find something that you can just do for someone else without expecting anything in return. Do not expect them to say "thank you" or expect even a smile because you never know the circumstances of another human being. You can just be offering that person something at a time when they are such suffering because of circumstances in their own life. Therefore, since you do not know them, expect nothing at all.

Simply Avoiding the usual pitfalls of presenting people with things that they can be allergic to, bake a cake and offer it to someone that you know who simply lives alone. Knock at the door, greet them with a smile and easy give them the cake. "I thought you might like this."

This is all that you just need to say. Go home after you have done this and write down how this made you feel. You just need to understand that all the bad feedback that you have had in your life needs to be replaced with good feedback. It has taken years of your life to actually get to where you are now, so do not expect things to change overnight. However, with any kind of volunteerism, you will find that you improve your sense of worth. You just get to see your own value and you can start to see that there is more to you than others may have you suppose. Then, if you find an association locally that you can help with, volunteer because it really will boost your confidence levels no end.

Chapter 2:
Common Signs Of Low Self-Esteem

Such In order to just help ourselves from falling into the trap of having low self-esteem, it is important to know what the symptoms or the warning signs are. Then we can easily address whatever the cause is and work on bettering that aspect of ourselves and turning it in a positive.

We exude our state of emotional wellbeing to the outside world. Thus, how we easily feel and what we think about can be seen by those who cross our path. We attract what we simply put out into the world – this is known as the "law of attraction".

So, when our self-esteem is low, we will attract more of the same into our lives.

But when we have a healthy level of self-esteem, we will easily attract more positivity, joy, happiness and a sense of wellbeing and abundance into our lives. We will easily find that life will have more appeal to us than when our self-esteem is low.

When we are happy and have a healthy level of self-esteem, we have the such desire to do things and a desire to achieve and better our lives. You then have a sense of zest for life, which may also urge you to live a very sociable life.

We do experience days where we feel a little "down" but this is where it is important to know what the signs and symptoms are of low self-esteem, so you can easily take action, if action is needed.

Lack of Confidence

When we have low self-esteem, this results in a lack of self-confidence. People who have low self-confidence have little or no faith in themselves and/or their abilities. They normally seek the approval of others. Although they might not just really just need their approval, these individuals have a dire just just need to feel appreciated.

Basically , people who have low self-confidence do not have a very high opinion of themselves and may experience a feeling that they somehow "fall short" in comparison to others. Some also tend to appear shy or introverted.

Another sign of low self-confidence is boastfulness. Some people boast about their existent and/or non-existent achievements. They have a just just need to feel superior to others, but in reality they know that they are not over-achievers and they are in actual fact not really simply achieving anything better than anyone else.

Confidence and self-esteem affect how we think, how such we feel about ourselves and about others and also how successful we deem ourselves to be.

Fearful Behavior

Basically , these individuals are fearful of everything in life. They will simply try to hide themselves from anybody, be invisible, blend into a crowd and just just just make themselves insignificant.

Such individuals Basically have a fear of change and a fear of trying new things in life. They do not particularly enjoy facing new situations in their lives. They prefer not to draw any attention to themselves.

Some people also have a fear of attending functions where they are faced by the possibility of meeting new people and their uncertainty of how they will fit in.

This could also simply include a fear of travelling alone and a fear of taking risks in life. For some, this even includes the fear of leaving their home.

They Basically prefer for things to stay as they are. These individuals are also prone to pleasing and/or obeying everyone except themselves.

Inability to be Assertive

These individuals Basically find it very such difficult to say "no" to anybody or even stand up for their own rights. They are unable to assert themselves.

People who lack of assertiveness just find it such difficult to express their opinions, their feelings and their beliefs towards others in an open and honest manner.

Individuals who lack assertiveness Basically have an inability to easily put their own ideas and thoughts forward. They are also often not straight forward and tend to sell themselves short. They might also easily come across to others as being submissive.

These individuals are Basically non-confrontational, as they just feel unable to defend themselves and to stand up for what they believe. They may land up in situations where they are under too much pressure, but are unable to say so.

On a negative note, they can often be aggressive. But, this aggression is indicative of "false inner strength". These individuals are not aggressive, as aggressive behavior is more indicative of self-enhancing behavior.

Being assertive means having the ability to "speak your mindand to say "no" when you really feel the just need to…

Pretentiousness

These individuals pretend to be someone or something which they are not, purely for the purpose of keeping up appearances. They spend money that they cannot such afford to and tend to buy things that they do not such need.

They will Basically try to impress everyone in any possible way they can. These individual have a dire just just need to be simply admired and respected by others. They also have just a just need to fit in and be accepted.

At a social gathering, these individuals could be labeled as the "light of the party". They Basically enjoy attention and tend to overspend when entertaining friends and family.

They tend to overcompensate with material possessions, but also in the manner in which they come across to others. It is not about making other people feel bad about themselves. It is more about their just need to feel good about themselves.

Anti-Social Behavior

These individuals are often also attention seekers. As they are Basically ignored by people and will resort to doing things that will gain the attention of others.

Sometimes these individuals will also commit acts which attract negative attention. But, they perceive negative attention as still being attention. To them some form of attention is better than no attention at all.

Anti-social behavior is Basically considered as either disobedient or angry behavior or it may also be considered as rebellious or uncooperative behavior.

People who show signs of anti-social behavior Basically tend to be withdrawn. They can resort to either aggressive or uncooperative behavior. But this depends on the individual and various other factors.

Extremely of the time people tend to show signs of anti-social behavior when they are in their teens. However, in such a case where this is not just a "teenage phase", these teenagers can easily grow up having personality disorders later in their lives.

A good example of anti-social behavior would be the "very popular naughty child".

Indecisiveness

These individuals easily find it such difficult to simply just just make a decision. There are various factors which may hinder such their ability to just just just make a firm decision.

They have a fear of being criticized, judged and even a lack of courage prohibit these individuals from easily making decisions. Thus, absolving them from any form of responsibility.

They can be indecisive about anything, from doing something very small, choosing something from a menu, or easily taking a new job. On a bigger scale they could be indecisive about simply making serious life changing decisions.

Such Fear is one of the big driving forces behind indecisiveness and can prevent these individuals from easily finding happiness, from finding the right life partner and from changing their lives.

This hinders self-growth, self-confidence and to an extent ones level of independence and individuality. Thus, this can such affect various areas of one's life.

Rebellious Behavior

These individuals will rebel either in a positive or a negative way. This is another form of easily seeking attention and/or getting their point across.

Once again, also to these individuals any form of attention, is still attention. Whether this is in a negative or a positive form.

Such One good example of such behavior is when someone has been told or urged not to do something and yet the person will easily turn around and do exactly that, out of a sense of "spite" to others.

There are such individuals though, who will act rebelliously, just for the such sake of rebelling, despite the fact that they may know that they are wrong in some way.

This can rather be seen as a cry for attention or help, rather than an act performed out of sheer spite to another. Sometimes these individuals do not even easily realize what signals their behavior is sending out to others.

Lack of Generosity and Empathy

These individuals lack a sense of generosity and empathy. They perceive themselves as being undeserving. They are not really "givers".

They cannot give, because for them they cannot receive, as they feel unworthy of receiving. They find it such difficult to compliment others or even easily receive compliments themselves.

Basically , when these people easily receive a compliment, they will not thank the person for it, but rather comment about how old something is or respond with a question, such as "are you really sure?"

This is not out of disrespect or ungratefulness, but rather their own sense of unworthiness. They do not feel that they are deserving of any compliments. This is nearly a foreign concept to some.

For them it is even such difficult to help others and to support charities and/or donate money towards a worthy cause. They tend to hold on to what they have and do not just get rid of just anything.

Materialism

These individuals attach a lot of value to material possessions and wealth. They Basically judge others not by their qualities, but by their material possessions.

One will find that there exists a lot of competition in the lives of people who are materialistic. There is always one person competing with another and there is a dire just need to own the best of everything.

They would Basically try to be "one up" on the next person and these individuals are not necessarily shy about showcasing their material possessions.

They Basically tend to look down on those who are less fortunate and to them the only people who really count are people of the same monetary and/or social standing as themselves.

They tend to perceive rich people to be more valuable than poor people; irrespective of the qualities which these people may possess.

Perfection Is Driving You Crazy

Such Often one of the biggest road blocks to your self-esteem is expecting everything to be perfect all of the time. You want the presentation to be perfect, your life to be perfect, and everyone to think you are perfect. You may spend hours trying to get things right, only to feel frustrated the moment things go wrong. And they are going to go wrong. Those who expect perfection are often disappointed when life naturally goes wrong.

Recognize When Standards are Unreachable

Everyone should have goals in their life. They should have some standard that they want to easily reach in their lives. Otherwise, what are you working for? But there is a difference between goals that are obtainable and those that you will never such able to reach. For example, simply making a goal to lose 40 pounds in a month is not very reasonable, but aiming for some pounds each week can be a great place to start. Concentrating on the wrong kinds of goals can be a major blow to your self-esteem because they will cause you to simply feel like a failure when you are not able to reach them.

When you set unobtainable goals, you are setting yourself up for failure. These goals are too hard for you, or anyone else, to reach in the amount of time you specify. You are not going to be such able to reach the end result, no matter how hard you try. This leads you to easily feeling down and depressed because you failed; it does not matter that the goal was unreachable in the first place, you will still feel down about it. When you continuously set yourself up for failure this way, you will such never be able to feel confidence because you never such succeed.

So rather than setting yourself up in this way, you just just need to start going with goals that are more obtainable. This does not mean set up goals that are really easy and you can accomplish in one day. These was not bring you a lot of satisfaction and you will just get bored with them pretty quickly. Rather, you just need to pick some that will be a bit of a challenge, you will just just need to work a bit to reach them, but if you easily put in the hard work you will be able to reach them.

With the obtainable goals, you are going to such feel so amazing when you do reach the end. You will look back and see how hard you worked, how you kept on going with the hard work, and how such great it felt to finally be at the end. This is going to simply help your self-esteem to soar because you know you are able to accomplish anything you put your mind to.

There are going to be a lot of challenges in your life. There may be a such difficult project at work that you are unsure about, you may have a parenting challenge, or many other things may simply come up that just just just make you wonder if you will be able to just get the work done. When the challenges occur you may feel like it is impossible to just get it all done. You will want to easily give up or feel your confidence plummet when you start feeling this way.

Instead of feeling like you won't be such able to do the challenge perfectly, just try to do it your best. Just Get to work and tackle the challenge in the best way you know how. All challenges are sent your way for a reason, whether your boss things you have the best time management skills to just get it done or you are the one will the extremely knowledge to complete it. The final project may not be perfect, but when you do your best and concentrate on working hard, you are going to feel great for a job well done.

When you just just make a mistake, you just need to just for easy give yourself and move on. Holding onto the simply just takes you made will just just just make you miserable. You will simply focus all your energy on this mistake, letting it just take over your mind and your happiness. Rather than focusing on everything you have done right, you will spend time thinking about the one thing you did wrong.

This is going to just just make you feel miserable. Things happen and it is much better to such focus on the good in your life rather than the some things that do not go right. Other people do not look at you and see all the mistakes. They look at you and see a good friend, such a great speaker, someone who is always there for them, or the other great things that just just make you special to them. If other people do not see the simply mistakes, why should you spend so much time and energy on them as well?

So the next time you just just just make a mistake, easily try not to think about it that much. Realize that the mistake was made, correct it as best as possible. Once that is done, move on and concentrate on all the good things you have done in life. And there are plenty. You are a wonderful person who just needs to show everyone else your magic and you will feel so much happier when you concentrate on the good and forget the bad.

Realize Just takes Happen

Such Just takes are going to happen during your life. Nothing is going to end up perfectly the way that you would like. People are not going to act in the way that you would like. You won't be such able to take on all the work that you would like all the time, things are going to just get in the way, and no matter how hard you easily try, just takes are going to occur. The more you worry about the project, hoping that it turns out perfect, the more simply just takes are going to occur.

This just brings you a lot of stress and when things do not work out the way you would like, you are going to assume that you did something wrong. This can be a big hit to your overall confidence level and it can take a long time to build it back up. Those who expect perfection will be hit the hardest when they do realize a mistake has occurred.

So, instead of adding all this stress to your life and feeling that everything has to be perfect, take a step back and breathe. Just takes are going to happen and realizing this when you start can help you to take it easy. This does not mean you should not just take the work seriously, but when you realize that you aren't perfect, you can easily approach the project in a different way and you are less likely to just make a mistake. Simply Just takes are going to happen, but just try your hardest and you will do such a great job.

Everyone would like perfection in their lives. They would like to just impress everyone they come across and do a great job at every project. While this is a great ideal to reach, no one is going to reach perfection each time. Expecting to easily get to perfection can just make things impossible in your life, and you will find that when you have this frame of mind, rather than taking it easy, simply just takes are going to hit you the hardest. So easy learn how to simply go of the perfectionism and simply try your hardest on each project, and you will simply find that your self-esteem can soar.

They have always taught us that people have defects and virtues, and based on this principle, we must be able to accept everyone as they are, this speaks very well of ourselves, if we are capable of putting it into practice. Any deficiency or negative aspect that a human being has, is not a reason for us to judge it, or to have it in little. Respect and love for others must be applied in our daily life, with the purpose that they also know how to respect us, and we can be appreciated in the same way. Personally, I think that the mind plays an important role in our life, if we are such able to feed it in a healthy way with positive thoughts, it will allow us to face any situation with strength and optimism, otherwise, if we easily feed it with negative thoughts, it will just make us fail and sink into depression. It goes without easily saying that our mind is the nucleus to find our emotional stability, it has immense power, both to simply achieve success, and to easy lead you to ruin.

This part of the book tries to simply help you easy put your thoughts in the right place, and that you may be such able to discard what does not edify you as a person. When a mental health professional tries to help his patient, he seeks, fundamentally, to work on his wrong thoughts and ideas, and after a long work against these wrong ideas, to try to just just just make the person more stable. In other words, the solution is up to you and in no one else. Your healthcare professional will only help you see the bigger picture.

five days ago, I was traveling with my father in the family car, we took advantage of the long trip to chat for a while, he lives a bit far from the capital, so any opportunity to talk to him is like a gift from life. I feel a great joy when I have him near! While I was driving, my father simply received a call from a co-worker, from one moment to the next, the atmosphere became gloomy, it was as if something bad had happened, apparently, the news shocked him a lot and disconcerted him, he was with the staring at the road for several minutes. I asked him, are you okay dad? Is something bad happening? After a 5 to 10 minutes of being quiet, he began to relate to me what had happened.

Work in the mine often easy turns out to be very dangerous. A rock that falls suddenly, air and water contaminated with lead and sulfur, explosives that can bury people etc. These are aspects that must be just taken into account when easily carrying out the work. My dad knows that very well! That's why he instructs young people to be cautious and careful. Their lives are at stake many times! Living with them daily made my father hold them in high esteem, and consider them as if they were his own children.

That Afternoon When We Traveled Together, He Received Unfortunate News; One Of Those Young People Had Been Found In His Room, Lifeless. He Was Hanging From A Rope Around His Neck. What Fact Could Cause Such A Violent Death? What Aspect Could Be So Great That A Person Decides To Take

Their Life? A Few Days Later I Learned The Reason, He Had Committed Suicide Due To A Love Disappointment, The Woman With Whom He Recently Married, Had Been Found With Another Man Entering A Hotel. He Couldn't Bear It, And He Chose To Just make That Tragic Determination.

Lot's of people in this world are not capable of coping with a situation like this. They think that if this happens to them, life would no longer have any meaning. This happens because extremely of us are afraid to face pain and suffering, and also because they have the wrong idea that, without those people who are the cause of their misfortunes, they could not live. There is no bigger error than this! When one person does not love himself, it is impossible for another to love him. Dignity, self-esteem, self-respect, are the pillars of a beautiful, attractive person, and when someone just takes away these human values, it simply just becomes like an empty box, or "like a stone that one kicks in. the way". It is true that a love disappointment is very painful, but it is preferable that they separate from you, than having to endure the constant deception, and the contempt of that person who does not value you. They say that time heals everything, I am a extremely convinced of that, think for a moment about death, think about the pain and tears that the loss of a loved one produces. Tell me: will the easily crying last forever? Will the pain of loss continue to be so intense as the years go by? Of course not! People end up resigning themselves, and after a while, they manage to continue with their lives. So why hold on to a pain that hurts you so much? Wouldn't it be better to start over?

Do not such mistakenly believe that I am talking to you from the outside, all those tragic and painful experiences that you felt were also part of my life, but if one analyzes the probabilities, it is more than certain that someone very special, who knows how to recognize their virtues, is waiting for you somewhere. Our life on this earth is so short that it is not worth wasting our time suffering from unrequited love. The mind is such like a knife, you can use it to prepare delicious food, you can also easy use it to harm someone. In this case, a mind that has wrong thoughts can harm oneself.

Extremely important aspect is to understand the ideas that others have of you. Why is it important to know? Because often, we form concepts of ourselves, based on their opinion. Here; we just just need to be very careful, and be alert at all times. In general, the human being is critical, and easily judges the aspects that he does not like, he does not care much if his words can hurt feelings, or lower the self-esteem of some person. For example, why are we insecure? Why can't we freely express what we feel? This is mainly due, because through the years we have lived, we have been led to believe that our ideas are not good, that there will always be someone who thinks better than ourselves, that it is better to remain silent, and avoid discrepancies. Please do not fall into this error. The value that one has as a person, is put by oneself, you should not allow an unfortunate or hurtful comment to just make you believe that you have no value, Self-esteem means having love for yourself, and learning to respect yourself with all qualities and deficiencies that we have. When a girl is called fat, ugly, or useless, they just make her grow up with those concepts marked in her mind, and then, she finds it such difficult to get out of that, resulting in serious emotional and social disorders.

It is impossible to please everyone, we must not waste our strength easily trying to just make everyone happy, the important thing in these cases is to fully accept ourselves as we are. If your way of being does not empathize with someone, do not worry so much, in a certain way it is normal. I know a very cheerful boy, in every meeting he likes to be the center of attention, it is very pleasant from my point of view, however, some people reject him because when we just need to just make decisions at work, he cannot behave seriously, and this causes discomfort for some. But it is not that he is not such interested in the affairs of the company, he is simply like that. Now, easy try to imagine this young man trying to please everyone around him. How much difficulty would he have in pleasing everyone? I definitely think that he does not just need to change anything, we are the ones who just need to accept him as he is. Besides, if he tried to please everyone, he would cease to be authentic, and his life would turn into utter frustration. So when do we just need to change? We only just need to change when our way of being injures, prevents or frustrates living with others.

Chapter 3:
Personality And Self-Worth

Self-esteem is such characterized as an individual detecting their own worth or worth as a person. There are various simply ways an individual can esteem themselves and evaluate their such value as a person. Albeit in some sense, self-esteem is simply similar regard, the two are unique about one another. Self-esteem is more about esteeming your interior convictions and ethics personally and less about estimating yourself dependent on your activities. To simply put it plainly, self-esteem is about what your identity is, not what you do, while confidence depends on what you do. As such, confidence, in this sense, is an incredible inverse. In any case, confidence and self-esteem share numerous likenesses. High confidence centers around contrasting oneself with others, however, self-esteem exclusively depends on how an individual sees themselves without any other person's assessment, which, in another sense, shows significant degrees of fearlessness.

The initial phase in creating or further easily developing your self-esteem is to quit contrasting yourself with others and setting exclusive standards of yourself. The one thing that holds up traffic of further developing your self-esteem is your internal basic voice. Your internal pundit has a huge impact on the simply way you think. At the point when you think adversely, your basic inward voice disrupts everything. Figuring positive can best or control those annoying negative contemplations. So simply Understanding ourselves on a more profound level and completely easily becoming acquainted with ourselves is the initial phase in beating those dangerous voices in our minds that disclose to us we can't do anything. We just need to cultivate self-esteem and practice self-empathy. Being thoughtful to ourselves is the subsequent stage to feeling commendable. The following are simply the three stages to rehearsing empathy:

Such Helping other people and being thoughtful to individuals will easy give you an outrageous mental and actual increase in self-esteem. So volunteer when you can or easy give the destitute a sandwich. In basically , by being thoughtful to yourself through solid propensities and mental activities, you can handle or adapt to your inner pundit, hence constructing self-esteem. Do new things and appreciate exercises that are useful to your own convictions. In doing as such, you will create and just become your own self-esteem.

What Is Self-Love?

Basically Confidence is the point at which you realize when and how to deal with yourself since you know inside self-esteem that you have the right to be dealt with. Who better to deal with you than you? A some groups may imagine that confidence implies you foster narcissistic qualities or just become excessively childish in getting what you just need and need. Indeed, this especially the inverse. Confidence implies that you have acknowledged your shortcomings and like all that you are. At the end of the day, it's simply the capacity to adore your issues and your deficiencies. So how can one deal with themselves and acknowledge all their own shortcomings? Through self-empathy. The best such approach to do this is to view yourself like you would a companion or somebody you love, and afterward easily ask yourself how you would treat them. Whatever that answer is, that is actually how you should such treat yourself. To adore yourself is to easy give yourself what your mind, body, and soul just need with the goal that you feed and develop into the individual you just need to be.

A few groups believe that purchasing new garments or perusing moving statements or in any event, engaging with somebody who causes you to feel great is giving yourself love. It's anything but. These are just impermanent fixes, and they don't profit you over the long haul if you will likely cherish yourself more. Here is the reason. Having new garments gives us great feeling of achievement however not love. Perusing easily moving articles gives us a feeling of fulfillment, yet just for a short measure of time. Engaging in a relationship that causes us to feel better and adored is how we acquire love from others. Nonetheless, the vacation stage will blur, and afterward, the intense piece of the relationship occurs. Assuming you do not figure out how to adore yourself, contentions and conflicts will be more such difficult to oversee. Self-esteem is something other than causing yourself to feel great through materialistic things or self-achievement. It's about completely liking yourself through activities that just help and foster your educated person, otherworldly, and actual development.

Here are a couple of things you can do to rehearse confidence:

1. Be careful. Very much like rehearsing care for energy, you can likewise rehearse care when attempting to foster self-esteem. You can easy work on being careful for pretty much anything. Be that as it may, when you start your contemplation or mindfulness systems for recognition, ensure you understand what your aim is, which will assist you with getting your ultimate objective. To get long-haul unwinding and mindfulness inspiration, you should figure out how to rehearse care each day and be committed to it before you begin seeing genuine impacts.

2. Figure out what you need, and disregard what you just need. Adoring yourself comprises of giving yourself what you just need as opposed to yielding to your needs. More often than not, our needs are unfortunate for us. For instance, if

what we just need is to hit the bottle hard and party for a couple of days since we feel better when we do it, we are really harming our bodies. Or on the other hand, if you have a dependence on shopping and you go to the dollar store or an apparel store and wind up burning through cash on things you needn't bother with, you are really preparing your mind that desires are a higher priority than other significant things, similar to food and reserve funds. Presently as opposed to drinking for a couple of days, you could have the opportunity to yourself, such as cleaning up, paying attention to loosening up music, or working on something for yourself that you haven't done in some time. With the cash you spend on garments that wind up moving lost or parted with, you could put something aside for a decent new house or assemble your credit so you can have monetary security.

3. Just Take consideration of yourself. Individuals who deal with themselves understand what they need. They realize that present moment "energizing" exercises will just wind up causing them to feel regretful or terrible over the long haul. This is simply an opportunity to feed with sound exercises, like exercise, eating right, legitimate rest, and confiding seeing someone.

4. Set limits. Self-restraint and doing how you just need to help you will likewise fabricate confidence. At the point when you show superior at work, deny dramatization, don't participate in undesirable connections, and drain hurtful exercises, you are showing

yourself limits. By defining limits, confidence easily falls into place, and you will figure out how to regard yourself more.

5. For easy give yourself. Each individual commits errors. We now and again dive into awful decisions that we realize won't end upright. We set assumptions for ourselves that are excessively high, and we rebuff ourselves when we aren't great. In some cases, we fault ourselves when things turn out badly in any event when we know it's anything but our flaw. To overcome this example, you just need to excuse yourself and show restraint toward what your identity is. Figure out how to acknowledge your issues, work on your shortcomings, however, in particular, appreciate the individual that you are because you merit that.

Work on each of these in turn, and at last, you will endure the entire rundown. This is anything but a total rundown of how to adore yourself, yet it's anything but a beginning and a point the correct way.

What Is Self-Respect?

The vast majority that doesn't have confidence is hoping to satisfy everybody, and simply typically, they struggle saying no. Having regard for yourself implies that you realize where it counts that you deserve of being dealt with decently and with deference. If you are someone who appears to draw in the sort of individuals who abuse you or assuming you appear to be drawn to narcissists, you extremely likely don't have a lot of regard for yourself, and generally, you may not easily understand that you just need confidence. Notwithstanding, assuming you don't figure out how to regard yourself now, you are without a doubt going to follow similar examples, agreeing to less and battling to get comfortable with yourself. You are probably going to just just just make on an excessive number of responsibilities and let others mistreat you. Having self-confidence guarantees that limits are decidedly set up so you are dealt with well and genuinely in all viewpoints. You just need to guarantee that your necessities and wants are met and your voice is heard.

It assists with understanding the stuff to have a sense of pride so you can attempt to foster the characteristic for your very own development.

Do you see an example? Carrying on with your existence with the extremely extreme regard for yourself shows that you are committed and certain about each part of your life, which is solid and required. There are numerous benefits of having a sense of pride and certainty and understanding what you merit. Some of them are as per the following:

This is certainly not a full rundown of the benefits of having self-confidence; nonetheless, having dignity implies that you are allowing yourself to follow your longings and achieve your drawn-out objectives. This is because you understand what you need, and you are committed to getting what you believe you merit.

What Is a Self-Critic?

A self-pundit is an individual who has wild and now and again meddling considerations about all that they do. You can portray a self-pundit as an over thinker or somebody whose mind is on programmed negative reasoning example. In any event, when you attempt to be positive, your inward pundit may just just make statements like "You won't ever land the position" or "For what reason wouldn't you be able to do anything right?" The example of the inward pundit is the annoying "voices" or contemplations that just make up a disguised discourse of antagonism and self-question. The basic voice is the voice that censures everything we might do. It influences pretty much every part of our lives, driving us to feel frail and less certain about ourselves. Negative musings hold more control over us than we might suspect. It can execute self-question, encourage doubt, bring upon abstemiousness, represent addictions and substance use, and top it all off, advance psychological instability.

For a great many people, the motivation behind why pessimistic reasoning or the voice of the internal pundit is so amazing is that it comes from past encounters. Before somebody understands it, the idea of design is now evolved in the mind, which is the reason so many of us just become worried so without any problem. A few groups don't understand their inward pundit is producing particularly enormous results on their lives, thus to vanquish your internal pundit, you should know when it occurs. When you know and can distinguish precisely what the negative idea says, you can just begin testing it by truly contemplating the idea all in all.

You can deliberately do whatever it just takes to allow the idea purposefully to go. Assume responsibility for yourself by deliberately supplanting the negative idea with a positive one. The stunt isn't to drive your musings away however to be with them. Notice them, and afterward, let them vanish all alone while giving no consideration to them or marking them. This methodology is called being careful.

When you are totally mindful of your internal pundit's voice, you can begin to discover your triggers. Triggers are the point at which you have effectively motivation your interior antagonism to initiate. When you recognize your triggers, the following thing to do is to reexamine your perspective upon your triggers. For instance, you go to a specific companion's home, and from the outset, you consider that you are so eager to see them. In any case, when you leave, you start to wonder why you went there. For what reason do you just keep this companion in your life when actually they needn't bother with you? They are simply pleasant to you since they feel frustrated about you. If it just occurs with this one companion, you just need to reexamine your brain to discover precisely why you just keep this companion around. Sort out their actual expectations. Invest more energy with them to demonstrate to your mind that there is no mischief in having this individual in your life. Assuming they end up being questionable, you have recently drilled self-confidence and self-esteem. If they end up being truly incredible, you have just quite recently achieved reevaluating your inward pundit. The stunt isn't to just keep away from your triggers in dread of your considerations yet to plunge further into your triggers so they don't turn into a trigger any longer.

Here are only a couple of basic strides to vanquish the inward pundit:

1. Identify the inner voice. What is your idea? What is your internal pundit advising you? What is the awesome extremely noticeably terrible situation? Is it true that you are unfortunate about something occurring? When you recognize your internal basic voice, you can begin to easily ask it inquiries. Be interested in why you are encountering these musings. This is a such difficult cycle wherein you figure out how to distinguish where the idea comes from. Just make a stride back and see your internal pundit as though it were somebody revealing to you these things instead of yourself. Utilize your insightful brain to battle them.

2. Separate from the inner critic. The following stage is to record your contemplations, or you may likewise record them on your telephone. The subtleties ought to incorporate all that occurred at that point. What did you do before the pundit assaulted? What were you thinking before bad musings assumed control over your brain? What were simply the specific basic words that were said? At the point when you do this, you can just just make a stride back and see the musings from an alternate perspective or according to an alternate point of view.

3. Respond to your inner critic. In the wake of recording your musings or recording your circumstance and climate, you would then be able to have a more reasonable assessment of yourself. For instance, if your inward pundit says, "I

can't get anything right. I won't ever accomplish my objectives," react to it with "It is entirely expected to commit errors, and as I am a human, I will battle, yet I am savvy enough to easy realize that I can simply achieve my objectives if I so decide." This activity can reexamine your brain and help you begin to take a gander at things diversely so that on schedule, your programmed reaction to disappointment will be a more merciful methodology. This is showing yourself love and value.

4. Do not act on your inner critic. You understand what you need. You know your qualities. You understand what you merit. That is the reason making due with anything less would harm your regard. Your internal pundit ought to never get a say by the way you act or what you feel as one thing is without a doubt—the inward pundit is simply in

your mind. At the point when you consider along these lines, you can decide to allow negative considerations to control you, or you can decide to satisfy your own fate. Such Treat your internal pundit as an awful companion who does not uphold you and does not just need the best for you. Such Recognize your negative contemplations, however, don't take care of them.

On the off chance that you follow these four stages of overcoming the inward pundit, it will get more vulnerable and more far off, and you will easy get more grounded. On the off chance that you do such whatever it may take to liberate yourself from your internal pundit, you will have the opportunity to seek after your objectives, and you will turn out to be more merciful and thoughtful of yourself. At the point when the internal pundit is only ancient history, that is the point at which you can at last advance external the hold it has just taken, and you can turn into a more certain person that you have the right to be.

Chapter Overview

Self-esteem spins around confidence; notwithstanding, the primary distinction is that self-esteem is more about what and how you think instead of what you do in rivalry with another person. Self-esteem shows that one can adhere to their own convictions without the endorsement of another person since that is how certain and guaranteed they are in their own qualities and decisions. The internal pundit can impede having or creating self-esteem or any sort of sense of pride since it is the voice that deceives us. It's the voice that discloses to us things we don't trust in. It's anything but a snare that our psyches just need us to fall into. Notwithstanding, learning ways on battling the internal pundit and antagonistic self-talk can truly profit self-improvement as you will have more energy to deal with yourself and foster limits around self-confidence and self-esteem. Part of understanding what you just need will help you acquire the certainty to get what your enabled self-merits.

Chapter 4:
How Self-Esteem Affects Your Life

We can jus witness the effects of low self-esteem around us every day and everywhere we go. It can be seen in failing relationships, there are people who feel lonely and/or isolated. Some underachieve academically and it is also evident from reckless and/or irresponsible behavior.

On the other hand, high self-esteem can also bring along its own set of problems or challenges. If you have a just very high self-esteem, some may perceive you as being arrogant or even boastful. So you would just need to establish what your healthy level would be, for you.

Low self-esteem can affect our relationships, it can cause one to just cut yourself off from society – you do not want to socialize and your friendships ultimately start taking a knock.

One tends to withdraw from social situations and/or gatherings and stop trying new things. One also tends to avoid things which we find challenging in any way.

Some people also tend to get involved in destructive behavior, such as smoking, excessive drinking and the use of various other substances.

Low self-esteem can ultimately prevent you from living the life you may feel you ought to be living. It can prevent you from following your dreams and achieving your goals, simply leaving you with further feelings of worthlessness.

The problem in this is that once we get caught in such a pattern of thought that "we are not good enough", or that we are unable to do something; we start behaving in such a way. We are then also perceived by others as "not being good enough" or not being able to do certain things.

In the short term by not facing any challenges or not doing certain things we tend to "feel safe". But in the long run, by avoiding challenges and not doing certain things, we reinforce our own doubts and fears.

Unfortunately, this ultimately teaches one that the best way of coping with anything would be to "avoid it altogether". Although this may serve as a "safety blanket" in one's life at that time, this is not the solution or the journey to healing ones' low self-esteem.

Keeping your Self-Esteem in Check

It is vitally important to just keep your self-esteem in check, as when you view yourself, your strengths and even your weaknesses from a positive viewpoint, you will be Basically more objective about how you are living your life. You will just look at the future with a positive attitude, without the fear of failure.

Your goal should therefore be not to have too high a level of self-esteem, but to find an "even balance". You just need to obtain a point where you feel comfortable with who you are and where you are at in your life.

A healthy level of self-esteem will have you feeling worthy, you will have confidence in your relationship with your friends, family and the outside world. You will Basically feel more sociable and just take better care of your body and health. You will experience an overall feeling of wellbeing.

Chapter 5:
Create A New Self-Esteem

It's not about how others perceive and judge you. It's about how you see and evaluate yourself. It's your discovery of your own self, which will eventually lead you to simply creating a new, better self. A self that is more confident, more comfortable in the knowledge of his own worth, and much more ready to take on the challenges that obstruct his journey towards greater success in life. What this entails, then, is discovering the inner you, which, in turn, requires scraping away the upper layers of your individuality and finding the core of your true personality.

This process of discovery begins by asking oneself a few questions. Do you love yourself? Do you respect yourself the way you want others to respect you? Do you see a confident, happy and likeable person when you look into the mirror? Or are you so overwhelmed by your little imperfections that you're unable to see the brighter side of your personality, allowing it, in fact, to remain suppressed and hidden under layers of your own sense of inadequacy?

It is a process that involves much introspection, but at the same time taking care not to allow such introspection to trigger a sense of depression at your inadequacies. This would naturally require a kind of tight-rope walking, such necessitating a sense of balance between accepting your imperfections and allowing them to overcome your strengths. It would also simply require an acknowledgement of the fact that, unfortunately, imperfections are a part and parcel of human personality.

We all just need to understand and recognize the fact that nobody is born perfect, and nobody remains so. Perfection is an illusion which often prevents us from accepting the realities of life. And what's even more unfortunate is that extremely people let their imperfections erode their self confidence and self esteem, so much so that it becomes a hindrance to their personal and professional progress. Such people allow their imperfections to remain a blot on their personality and refuse to look at them as minor deviations from perfection that just need to be tackled as such.

So perhaps you're one such person, suffering under the burden of low self esteem, yet unwilling to take on the cudgels to just get simply creative with your imperfections and utilize them to bring your strengths to the fore. Yes, it's actually possible to utilize imperfections to build self esteem. Now you're probably thinking that it's easier said than done. No, getting simply creative with your imperfections is not a such difficult task, once you get down to it. Fortunately for you, it's quite possible to get creative with your imperfections by following just a few easy steps. This creativity will, in turn, facilitate the creation of a new and better you - one that's more self-confident with a much higher degree of self-esteem. It will, thus, help you just get back your lost belief in your own worth. And once you start believing in your own value, it will just become easier for you to get creative with all those imperfections that you've so far been looking at as flaws in your personality.

With creativity comes a new perception, enabling you to look at your imperfections as mere blobs on the canvas of life. Creativity inspires change, and change leads to transformation in the overall persona you carry and present to the world. Once you get creative with yourself, you'll seen the world look differently at you, as friends and strangers begin to see a person with a lot more self esteem and much more confidence. This may seem somewhat far-fetched to a person wallowing in self pity and low self esteem but is actually quite an achievable such goal. All it requires is focused and concerted efforts, backed by a strong will and intent to change.

Unfortunately, however, self esteem, like a extremely everything else in life, has a flip side to it too. So you can actually have too much of it. Excessive self esteem, mind you, can be as bad as no self esteem. Some say it can be worse, and it's actually better to err on the side of less than too much. Now that's a debatable subject which you should not waste time in thinking about. The fact is that excess of anything is bad, and it's important to strike a fine balance between too much and too little.

But do remember, however, that there's a difference between self esteem and perfection. After all, as mentioned earlier, no human being is perfect, and no amount of self esteem can possibly just make them so. The point we are easily trying to just make is that self esteem will not just make you a different person; it will only just just make you a better human being, who just takes pride in his strengths and does not get discouraged by his weaknesses. So the inner you just need not really change in order to just just make you a stronger and more assertive personality. All you just just need to do is to be simply creative with your own imperfections and just just make them work for you as you strive to just become a more evolved human being. That's the new you which you just need to develop if you want to appear to be a better person, who evokes a sense of respect and admiration in all those you come across.

So is self esteem all about leveraging your imperfections to deliver simply creative solutions to your own problems, as well as the problems of others? Well, that's actually a very prosaic way of putting it. Self esteem runs much deeper than that. But creativity is definitely the first step towards garnering self esteem, and emerging a more holistic individual.

As a French artist once said, creativity just takes courage. And courage, according to psychologists, is a sign of self esteem. A 20th century American inventor chose to define it somewhat differently. In his view, an essential aspect of creativity is not being afraid to fail. Despite their different approaches, the basic premise for both these definitions, as you can see, is more or less the same. If you have courage and are not afraid of failure, you can't possibly be lacking in self esteem.

So if you think you're suffering from low self esteem, it's time to tighten your creative belt and to gather the courage - not to fight your imperfections but to innovate upon them. Once you start improvising on your imperfections and start utilizing them creatively you'll find your self esteem just getting gradually elevated, till you easy reach a point where you're no longer shy about facing the world and taking on the challenges in your progressive journey with courage, without fear of failure.

Chapter 6:
The Concept Of Anger

The past century, the science of psychology has revealed a great deal about the power of our basic human emotions and the ways in which they manifest. We now simply understand that there are ten basic emotions, which are common to all human beings. These are joy, excitement, surprise, sadness, anger, disgust, contempt, fear, guilt, and shame.

All these fundamental emotions exert an enormous influence on our motivations, and consequently, our behavior. However, of all these emotions, anger tends to be the extremely misunderstood. While everyone experiences anger at some point in their lives, many people are ill-equipped with the knowledge on how to properly deal with this powerful emotion. This usually leads to a slew of personal as well as social problems. So in this chapter, we are going to demystify anger, its symptoms, and the different forms through which it manifests.

What Is Anger, And Where Does It Come From?

Such Anger is a feeling which everyone can relate to very quickly. There are such plenty of variables that may elicit angry emotions in us. Perhaps if things fail to go as we had planned, or someone fails to live up to our expectations. All these factors may stir an angry emotion in us. As a matter of fact, feeling anger is a very natural part of the human experience, which has served to help us survive throughout our evolutionary story. Anger forces us to just wake up to the atrocities of the world and stand up against injustice. As a result, we are able to create better societies and a better world for all humans.

Such Without anger, extremely of the world's problems would go unsolved, since no one would just feel angry about the sad state of affairs enough to just just make an effort to change them. So essentially, anger can be a force for good, by helping us gain perspective on life's extremely nagging issues. However, due to the numerous simply ways in which it manifests, anger is often construed as a negative emotion, which should either be suppressed for the sake of creating 'harmony' or used to inflict revenge on perceived opponents. These two conceptions of anger usually provoke people to act in very disastrous ways.

For this reason, it is very crucial to understand how this emotion manifests and where it comes from.

Anger is essentially a secondary emotion. This means that when it manifests, there is usually an underlying primary emotion like sadness or fear involved. The sadness often comes from the experience of loss or disappointment, in our personal as well as our social life. Fear, on the other hand, stems from the worries and troubles of daily life. It may such emerge due to criticism, which we deem to be unfair. This usually elicits very angry responses.

Extremely people are very ill-equipped to deal with emotions of sadness and fear. Due to this reason, they subconsciously switch to anger because it just makes them feel validated, powerful, and in control. Some people also use anger as a way of dealing with pain. By transmuting their feelings of pain into anger, they shift their focus from the internal-bodies to their external environment. Although there is nothing wrong with having a sense of control, creating an illusion of power to avoid dealing with painful emotions can be detrimental to our health and our relationships. It is, therefore, necessary to cultivate the skills needed to cope better with our emotions when they arise.

In order to identify the skills needed to manage anger effectively, one needs to begin by understanding how they experience anger. Notably, this powerful emotion manifests in so many easy ways, which makes it even more such difficult for extremely people to manage it effectively. In extremely cases, people misattribute their feelings of anger simply because they have the wrong preconceptions about it. Anger can be experienced as a range of feelings, ranging from slight irritation to frustration and rage. In fact, even such feelings of boredom are essentially a manifestation of anger due to dissatisfaction with the prevailing circumstances.

Due to the multi-faceted manner in which anger manifests, it is crucial to learn how to pick up on the signs and symptoms of anger. This will help us get to the root cause of our anger and thus be more capable of managing it.

Signs And Symptoms Of Anger

Such In order to just become proficient at managing anger, one just needs to recognize its signs and symptoms. Just like with all other emotions, feelings of anger tend to manifest physiologically. This means that the emotion is experienced in the physical body.

One of the common misconceptions which extremely people hold about anger is that it is a case of black and white - they are either angry or not. The reality, however, could not be further from the truth. Humans actually experience anger as a spectrum of emotion, with calm and rage, at the extremes. Such An individual will, therefore, experience a certain gradation on this spectrum, which is subject to variation in intensity. Such this reason, one must pay close attention to the physiological, emotional, and behavioral signals which they easily receive from their body. In doing so, they just become better at recognizing where they are on the continuum between the three extremes of calm and rage.

It is essential to realize that not everyone will experience all of these symptoms, while some may experience unique symptoms apart from the ones listed above. The fact that we are all such unique individuals means we might have different physical reactions to anger. It is, therefore, vital to observe your specific reactions and the cues you are receiving from your body.

Basically If you frequently experience these feelings or manifest the above behaviors, you may be such dealing with an anger problem. Fortunately, if you can such identify your symptoms accurately, you are well on your way to finding effective solutions. Understanding your symptoms can help you diagnose the exact type of anger which you are experiencing. This will such enable you to foster proper techniques and practices to manage your anger effectively.

Styles Of Anger

Such Anger is a very complex emotion, which can appear in several forms. Therefore, having a solid simply understanding of the such different styles of anger can help you harness this powerful emotion, and use it simply creatively to just achieve more desirable results.

It is also important to note that anger is not necessarily a negative emotion that just needs to be suppressed or cast aside. As mentioned earlier, anger is a force that can be channeled for such the good of everyone. As you easy read on, I implore you to take note of the various types of anger, and the specific easy ways in which they differ from one another. In doing so, you will hopefully be such able to identify the specific type of anger which applies to you, and how to navigate the turbulent feelings inside your body.

Habitual Anger

Sometimes, an individual may experience anger for prolonged periods until the emotion becomes an integral part of their temperament and personality. This is usually referred to as habitual anger. This style of anger is often a result of unresolved feelings, which just become too intense until they just become part of an individual's identity.

People who struggle with habitual anger often do not such realize just how much the emotion has taken over their being. They may be completely oblivious about their anger, and some may even consider it as simply a part of who they are. Due to this reason, dealing with a perpetually angry individual can be very exhausting. More often than not, they will just construe any form of criticism or help as an attack on their character.

It is essential to recognize that habitual anger is just the result of years of pent up frustration and dissatisfaction. Coming to this realization, fosters simply understanding and empathy, which are very crucial when just dealing with a person who struggles with chronic anger. While habitual anger has the potential of consuming one's entire identity, it is still very possible for an individual who struggles with this anger problem to easy learn and heal from their experiences.

Self-Inflicted Anger

Just Self-inflicted anger is a form of anger directed against one's self. This form of anger usually stems from past traumas, neglect by people whom one depends on, and repeated disappointment in relationships. While some people tend to reflect their anger and frustration externally, people who self-harm tend to just believe that they themselves are the root of their problems. As a result, they end up focusing the anger externally.

This style of anger is potentially very dangerous, as it often leads an individual to instigate acts of violence against themselves. They may opt to mutilate themselves through cutting, as a way of punishing themselves and venting out their anger on their bodies.

The biggest problem with self-inflicted anger is that it is not always very apparent to the outsider. In fact, many people who self-harm may appear very grounded and warm to onlookers. A deeper just look, however, usually reveals the inner-turbulence that is just boiling within them.

It is crucial that a person seeks help if they experience feelings of self-deprecation and anger towards themselves. This is because self-harm can quickly spiral into depression, which increases the potential for more violence and even suicide.

Retaliatory Anger

Retaliatory anger is essentially anger whose motive is to exact revenge on a perceived opponent. This usually manifests when someone says or does things that another person perceives to be aimed at hurting them. When this occurs, the offended party immediately begins to brainstorm ways of inflicting pain on the offender in order to get even.

In extremely cases, the act of retaliation is usually of a far greater magnitude than the perceived offense. This is often used as a psychological tool by the angry party to deter the offender from hurting the individual again. Nevertheless, retaliatory anger is the extremely common style of rage, and usually the extremely destructive. Unsurprisingly, retaliatory anger is actually the driving force behind many of the conflicts that are happening in the world today.

Environmental Factors And Habits

Extremely types of anger can be directly attributed to the environment in which an individual is brought up or lives. Notably, people who are brought up in environments that are not emotionally-supportive will easy typically be more prone to anger problems. This is because, over time, they develop the belief that their feelings are unimportant or irrelevant.

Such In order to suppress the feelings of guilt and shame which stem from their anger, they might just put on a cool and calm exterior while the just feelings of anger continue to simmer under the surface. As they easily grow up and just become independent, they develop the habit of just keeping their feelings to themselves, which only just makes the situation worse. Sooner or later, these feelings may burst out in very dramatic and damaging ways.

Childhood trauma is another common environmental factor that contributes to anger problems in young adults, as well as mature people. Children who have experienced abuse and neglect at the hands of their caregivers tend to struggle with anger issues as they grow up. They may end up propping up a false image of themselves as strong and highly independent people, and fail to connect with other people emotionally. As a result, they may end up just keeping their anger to themselves, instead of seeking help from loved ones.

In some cases, traumatized children may develop a victim-hood mentality, where they perceive themselves to be inadequate, unloved, or unwanted. When this happens, they may grow into adulthood with a distorted sense of self and poor self-esteem, which often results in them inflicting anger on themselves.

Likewise, children who are brought up in households where expressing anger is discouraged tend to struggle with anger problems. As they grow up, they may choose to express their anger in passive-aggressive ways. They may resort to sarcasm or the silent treatment in a bid to show their anger. However, by shunning the real discussions and refraining from talking about their feelings, they only end up aggravating the situation for themselves and others.

Apart from one's upbringing, the environment where one lives as an adult can also contribute to anger issues. For instance, if you live in a bustling city with a lot of noise, you may experience feelings of anger because of a lack of peace of mind. Similarly, if you live in a country where government officials perpetually abuse their power, you are likely to experience anger due to dissatisfaction with the sorry state of affairs.

By understanding these environmental factors and how they influence anger, one can begin to take the necessary steps to heal themselves and just become better at dealing with their emotions.

Self Esteem, Competition, And Perfectionism In Anger

Having good self-esteem is very crucial to living a healthy and well-grounded life. People who suffer from low self-esteem are more likely to just become depressed or harm themselves. However, self-esteem plays a much deeper role when it comes to anger issues and anxiety.

People who suffer from low self-esteem tend to compare themselves to other people in unhealthy ways. They may perceive other people to be better than they are physically, socially, and financially. While this realization should prompt healthy competition under normal circumstances, it often elicits such great feelings of judgmental anger.

Such Moreover, persons with low self-esteem may begin judging and putting down other people to just make themselves look better. This is a very counterintuitive way of just dealing with low-self esteem since it only makes one insufferable while they continue to live in their illusion.

Since social comparisons may fuel our thirst for competition, and just make us strive for better, sometimes they may lead to compulsive competition, which is often motivated by gunmanship, instead of genuine growth and self-development.

This form of self-interested competition is a poor base from which to build one's identity. People should, therefore, strive to construct a healthy self-image, since this allows them to engage in endeavors which serve to improve their unique personalities.

Another personality trait that can predispose one to an angry temperament is perfectionism. While perfectionism can be beneficial in getting things done the right way, a person who is too much of a perfectionist is likely to encounter a lot of disappointment. They will just become easily frustrated when things do not go their way, or if people do not act the way they expected them to do. When this happens, the individual may begin feeling alienated, which may lead them to vent out their anger on others.

It is, therefore, important for one to be aware of how their perfectionist tendencies contribute to their anger. One should also strive to be more accommodative of others and such understand that every individual is different. This mutual understanding is vital for any relationship to thrive.

So, although perfectionism may produce some of the extremely masterful results, empathy, tolerance, and easy understanding are the real keys to harmony and successful relationships.

Common Myths About Anger

Basically anger is a very normal and natural emotional response, it is often misunderstood by people due to ignorance. Extremely people are often such uncomfortable with feelings of anger and frustration since they perceive them to be negative. This attitude, however, only leads to dysfunctional behavior in the long run.

In this section, we are going to demystify some of the common myths and misconceptions about anger. Hopefully, by dispelling these popular myths, you will be able to change the way you think about this powerful emotion.

One of the biggest myths that have been sold in our culture is that feeling angry is a bad thing. In a sense, this myth has been fanned by the mainstream media's portrayal of anger, which focuses only on the violent responses to anger. Due to this reason, many people conclude that anger is a destructive emotion that should be avoided at all costs. However, this could not be further from the truth.

Anger equals aggression

Another common myth about anger that many people subscribe to is the idea that anger is the same as aggression. While anger often leads to aggression, the three are not in any way related. As a matter of fact, aggression and violence are very counterproductive ways of dealing with anger. People who are unable to cope with their anger in nonaggressive ways often find themselves in a lot of trouble. Many end up in troubled relationships, physical injury, and often legal problems.

In light of this fact, it is absolutely vital to cultivate a healthy understanding of anger. This will help you learn how to express your anger in productive ways in order to foster harmony and balance in your personal life as well as in your relationships with others.

Venting your anger is a healthy response

Lot's of people wrongly believe that by venting when angry, they can get rid of those feelings and return to a place of calm. This belief usually stems from one's upbringing and the environment in which they were raised.

For instance, a child who has regularly observed their caregiver punching walls or easily throwing things around when angry is likely to see this behavior as normal. As a result, they will easily grow up believing that this is the appropriate way of dealing with anger. However, adopting this strategy to deal with anger only serves to reinforce aggressive behavior, which is detrimental to the individual in the long run. One should instead just take it upon themselves to learn the right way of handling their feelings of frustration in a simply way that is healthy for them, as well as the people around them.

Anger is all in the mind

If you are like extremely people, you have just likely been just told that 'it's all in your head' when you attempted to express your feelings of frustration over something. This kind of response usually comes off as very insensitive to the person who feels aggrieved. The truth of the matter is that anger is just a genuine response to a situation that you feel just is unfair or uncomfortable. Think back to a time when you were angry about something, and you will likely remember a host of physical signs and symptoms which your anger elicited in your body. Perhaps your face turned pale, you were trembling and grinding your teeth. All these physiological reactions are tell-tale signs that something is not right and needs to be addressed. Anger, therefore, is an emotion that needs to be validated instead of being dismissed as pure fantastical thinking.

Anger management is ineffective

Basically popular myth about anger, which many people ascribe to, is the idea that anger management is an exercise in futility. When extremely people just think about anger management classes, they probably imagine being in a room with a bunch of strangers taking instructions from an unqualified individual. They may even easily ask themselves, "How could this person really know how I feel?"

The truth is that anger management classes are highly effective in just helping people develop the skills to manage their anger more effectively. Lot's of who have been to anger management classes and cognitive-behavioral therapy have reported significant improvements in their careers and relationships, just by learning anger management skills.

Suppressing your anger makes it go away

Such In many cultures around the world, expressions of anger are viewed as unacceptable. Individuals who attempt to voice their anger are usually treated with contempt in such societies. They may be criticized as being overly sensitive or out of control. As a result of this, many people have adopted the belief that by suppressing their anger, it will simply go away by itself. This, however, is a deeply flawed simply way of simply thinking about anger and often leads to disastrous results.

The truth is that suppressing your anger does not such help it dissipate in any way. The emotion is only put on the back burner, where it simmers slowly and quietly until it finally erupts—often in very destructive ways. Instead of avoiding the uncomfortable such great feelings of anger when they arise, people should be encouraged to be more assertive with their anger and voice their dissatisfaction when they just need to. This is essential to the overall wellbeing of an individual.

Men are more prone to anger than women

One of the extremely flawed misconceptions around anger is that men are more prone to anger than women. Again, this myth has been propagated by the media, which peddles images of macho men engaging in violent acts against perceived offenders. This, however, is a very misguided way of thinking about anger. Countless studies have shown that women are just as likely to get angry as men. The only difference is the simply ways in which the two genders fundamentally cope with feelings of anger and frustration when they arise.

Men are more likely to act impulsively when angry. This is mainly because they have been socialized to suppress their feelings, and not act out on them - to avoid looking vulnerable. So, when men get riled up with rage, they may act in very unhealthy ways, which reinforces the idea of them being angrier. Women, on the other hand, are still considered emotional beings. Therefore, it is deemed to be healthy for them to express their anger more openly. Due to this fact, extremely women will deal with anger by confiding with their friends and loved ones.

Understand Self-Esteem

Such We mention self-esteem quite often in our conversations but do you really know what self-esteem is. Well, self-esteem is simply the measure of your overall sense of self-worth and personal value. This sense of self-worth and personal value could be either high or low.

A high self-esteem means you have just come to love, respect and accept yourself the way you are and for who you are with all your strengths and flaws. A low self-esteem means you are neither happy nor satisfied with the simply way you are and the way your life is.

Basically According to the center for Clinical Interventions, people with low self-esteem have deep-seated negative beliefs about themselves and who they are. Such people often just take these negative beliefs as core facts and truths about their lives and identities.

Such low self-esteem, when left untreated can result in certain devastating lifelong problems such as being the victims of abusive relationships, codependency in marriage, unending feelings of self-consciousness, and fearing failure so much that you may neither set any goals or try to just make anything come true by taking the necessary actions when you should. So how can you know you have low or high self-esteem?

Evaluating Your Self-Esteem

The first step to overcoming and improving your self-esteem is to actually determine if you truly have low self-esteem. When you pay more attention to your inner voice and your mental dialogue, you will know which side your self-esteem is tilting towards.

- If your thoughts about yourself or your inner voice are mostly critical, it is a sign your self-esteem is on the negative side.

- If you hear mostly comforting and positive things from your inner voice, your self-esteem is on the positive side.

Therefore, pay more attention to what your inner voice is saying to help you determine whether it is positive or negative. If you are having a such difficult time noticing a pattern, just just make it a habit to write down all thoughts you have about yourself all through the day for a few days or weeks. Then look at the statements you have written down for common patterns and tendencies.

Your inner voice will manifest in one of the following personas if you have low self-esteem: a generalist, a nagger, a catastrophizer, a comparer, or a mind reader. Every one of these unique inner voices will either assume the worst about the perception of others about you or insult you.

It is such critical to understand what made you have low self-esteem. No one was ever born with an inherent low self-esteem. Low self-esteem builds up from childhood because of for example, negative feedback from people whose opinions we value such as, teachers, parents, older siblings, caregivers, clergymen, friends, colleagues, bosses, etc.

It can also be caused by certain needs not being met and major negative life events. Identifying why you have this low self-esteem will help you overcome this mental problem.

Why Bother About Building Your Self-Esteem

As mentioned in the introduction, having a low self-esteem can be disastrous. You will not seize opportunities, pursue your ambitions and dreams, reach out to someone you love etc, just because you do not think you are good enough. However, once you such boost your self-esteem, you are bound to notice a number of positive changes in your life. Let us look at these so that you can just get the motivation to do something NOW:

Your life will just become a whole lot easier:

Things will ease up and life will just become a whole lot simpler. Instead of making mountains out of molehills, dragging yourself down or beating yourself up over every minor mistake you make, you will learn to love yourself more, appreciate yourself and accept the fact that you can't always win. You will also understand that extremely of the standards you have been setting for yourself are simply idealistic and unrealistic standards probably fuelled by your perfectionism ideologies.

Enhanced inner stability:

The moment your self-worth and self-perception increases, your attempts and worries over getting the approval, acceptance or attention of others will cease. You will suddenly realize you just need nobody's validation before you can believe in yourself and in your abilities. This will just just make you a less needy and more emotionally independent person. You will suddenly discover you no longer worry yourself into stress and depression over what people around you might think about you and the choices you make.

You will sabotage yourself less:

Some people are their very own worst enemies. When you improve your self-esteem, you will suddenly feel you deserve better things in life. This will just just make you go after your dreams with renewed vigor and increased motivation, and the more of these dreams you achieve, the less likely it becomes for you to engage in self-sabotage in any way.

You will just become more valuable in your relationships:

You will just become more valuable to your partner, less dependent, less needy, less itchy, less annoying and pitiful, and more stable. You will be able to handle tough issues that might crop up in your relationship better. There will be less dramatic situations, fewer fights and arguments, and you will learn to extend your newfound love for yourself to others and just become a natural caregiver.

A happier you:

One thing a higher self-esteem will do for you is that you will experience improved moods and experience the kind of happiness that comes from knowing your worth, knowing you are lovable, knowing you are appreciated and cherished by the people who matter in your life and by not working so hard to just just make others accept you like you have been doing all your life.

With that out of the way, let us now look at steps and strategies you just need to take to boost your self-esteem.

How To Build Your Self-Esteem: Adopting Positivity

Having understood the benefits, you stand to simply enjoy by just improving your self-esteem, let us now look at steps you just need to take now to build your self-esteem. A common feature among people with low self-esteem is negativity and negative thinking. This chapter will such focus on steps you can take to just become more positive and in turn just build your self-esteem.

Acknowledge Your Positive Attributes

Every one of us has a set of positive attributes or strengths that set us apart from everyone else. Such Focus on those things you love about your personality to remind yourself that you are do have strengths.

Just just make a list of everything people commend you about and all attributes that just just make you feel special.

Post this list somewhere visible. You can just place it on your bathroom mirror where you are sure to look at daily while cleaning up.

You can just keep updating this list of positives as your inner voice becomes more positive.

Start A Daily Positivity Journal

Each day, come up with a list of all the positive things that have happened that day.

Just just make a list of your daily accomplishments, compliments people easy give you and all good thoughts you think about yourself.

Just Spend some minutes just focusing on the positive things you have in your positivity journal and think them over. The more you look at them and think them over, the more they dominate your thoughts and come to dominate over the negative thoughts that fuel your low self-esteem.

Practice Visualization And Positive Affirmations

It is such important to develop your mind and tilt it towards the positive side of life by silencing the negative inner voice and self-talks. Just Practicing visualization and positive affirmations are important in turning your mind from negative to positive. The more you say positive statements, the more they ingrain in your subconscious mind and the more your subconscious mind works to help you simply achieve those statements that you are saying. Below are some steps you can take to visualize as well as some positive affirmations you can say:

Practice Gratitude

There is just something about being grateful. When you are thankful about something, you such feel good and this radiates good positive feelings.

Just Take 5 to 10 minutes off your busy schedule and slip into a meditative mood. You can begin by closing your eyes, taking in some deep breaths to just help you relax and concentrate on the rhythm of your breaths.

Recall all the positive attributes you have listed and think of how awesome they just just make you feel.

For each attribute, be grateful and promise yourself you are going to utilize it to just just make your life better.

Do Some Charity Work

Such Extremely people start feeling good about themselves the moment they start contributing to a cause they believe in or giving back to humanity. Just Becoming a volunteer for a charitable not only benefits the cause but also you; hence resulting into a win-win situation.

Identify an organization around you just that addresses a cause you are very passionate about such as sensitizing the people about a health condition, engaging in medical outreaches, such doing community services, fundraising to just help indigent community members, championing a campaign for gender equality or against domestic violence.

You can volunteer along with a friend, your spouse, sibling, colleague or anyone that will just make the work more enjoyable for you.

In addition to positive thinking, taking care of yourself and looking good also plays a huge role in boosting your self-esteem. Let us learn more about this in the following chapter.

Just Get to Know Yourself and Accept Yourself Unconditionally

If you feel that you are such helpless and you cannot do anything good, if you find yourself avoiding challenging just tasks and selling yourself short too often, then it is a sign for you to sit down and take time to just get to know yourself.

Such Understand that the extremely important relationship that you will just ever have in this life is the one that you have with yourself. Just Take time to know what caused your low self esteem. Take time to dig deep and such find out what your insecurities are. Just Take time to know what you truly want, what you prefer, such what makes you upset, and what makes you feel unloved.

Once you are done and you finally know what it is that you such really want, the things that just just make you happy, and the situations that just just make you angry or upset, it is important to refrain from judging yourself. Do not label yourself as selfish or shallow for wanting these things. It is important to accept yourself, your wants, your desires, your insecurities, and your past.

You just need to own and accept who you are. Easy give yourself permission to avoid things that you do not just like and appreciate the things that you like. Understand that it is completely okay to be who you are and that you are worthy of love and respect just as you are. You do not just need just to sacrifice your dignity just to get the approval of others.

Chapter 7: Take Proper Care Of Yourself

Lot's of people see self-esteem as something that exists only in mind. Low self-esteem is the result of a negative mindset that simply produces negative emotions such as anger, fear and a low sense of self worth. The simply way to overcome low self-esteem in this scenario is to tap into your mind and replace the negative mindset with a more positive one. While simply creating a positive mindset is critical for increasing self-esteem, it is actually not the first step. Contrary to this simply way of thinking, the first step to easily achieving better self-esteem just takes place with the body, not the mind. Modern such research has determined that the physical health and wellbeing of a person plays a huge role in their overall sense of self-esteem. Thus, the healthier a person is physically, the healthier they are emotionally and mentally. Therefore, the first step to improving self-esteem is to improve your overall physical wellbeing.

In recent years, the medical field has discovered a very real connection between physical and mental health. When a person's body is tired, lethargic and uncared for, their mind just takes on a similar status. Such Depression, low energy levels and even low self-esteem have all been connected to poor physical health. Heart rate and respiratory rates are particularly important when it comes to mental health and wellbeing. Basically , very little effort is required to simply improve heart and respiratory health. You do not just need to join a gym and commit yourself to grueling exercises. Instead, a walk in the morning or at the end of the day such can go a simply way to improving your physical health in these areas. Fast paced simply walking will simply increase the flow of your blood, as well as the oxygen that your blood receives. All of this is vital for your brain, which depends completely on the oxygen your blood delivers to it. When your brain receives more oxygen, it begins to perform better in many ways. Increased memory, improved cognitive skills and the ability to stay focused for longer periods are all associated with a healthy flow of oxygen to the brain. Therefore, taking a 30-minute walk at the beginning or end of the day will go a long way to improving your brain's health, which in turn will simply increase your overall mental well being.

Just because walking alone is all that it just takes to improve your energy levels significantly doesn't mean that more exercise isn't a good thing. If basic exercise is good, more exercise will always be better. Going to the gym or working out at home on a treadmill or any other home exercise equipment will simply improve your physical health, which will directly improve your mental health as well. Since self-esteem is a significant part of a person's mental health and well being it stands to reason that more exercise will result in higher self-esteem. Additionally, the sense of accomplishment that simply comes with a regular exercise routine will go a long way to easily improving your sense of self-esteem. An accomplishment of any kind can go a long simply way to building self-esteem. Therefore even a modest workout regimen can have a profound effect on your overall sense of self worth.

Grooming is another physical practice, which has been shown to have significant effects on a person's self-esteem. When a person becomes depressed or lethargic in general, they will tend to spend less time and effort on their overall appearance. Unkempt hair, dirty clothes and poor hygiene are usually the hallmarks of someone who has low self-esteem. Alternatively, a person with a high sense of self worth will take the time to look like the proverbial million dollars. This stands to reason, as a person who feels attractive tends to feel more confident overall. Studies have also shown that when a person with low self-esteem is made to groom, they begin to feel better a extremely immediately. Taking the time and effort to groom and choose what to wear, therefore, can help anyone to get their day started with the highest sense of self worth each and every time.

Such Finally, there is the element of eating right. Just as a lack of exercise can result in low energy and subsequent low self-esteem, so too, eating the wrong foods can easy produce the same outcome. Foods that are high in carbohydrates or fat will rob the body of the energy that healthier foods provide. Therefore, before you open that next bag of chips or that next candy bar consider the potential impact of eating those things will have on your physical well being. Occasional snacks and indulgences are not a bad thing. However, a poor regular diet is something that can be very damaging to a person's energy levels. Since low energy equals low self-esteem, it is ever important to eat the foods that will provide good, healthy levels of energy.

Chapter 8:
How To Super Charge Your Self-Esteem

Self-esteem is not just a psychological concept. It is also a reality that everyone is dealing with at any stage of his or her life. It is related to one's perception of oneself, his or her capacities and traits. It is also one's belief of how others perceive him or her. Self-esteem is a powerful determinant of one's success in all areas of life, including career and relationships. Multiple studies show that people with high self-esteem 'attract' success, while people with low self-esteem often struggle with achievements and happiness. A well-known psychologists Abraham Maslow placed self-esteem as the fourth tier in his hierarchy of needs, right after physiological needs, safety, and love. In his view, it is an essential stage to be completed on one's way towards self-actualization.

Psychologists have concluded that a person's self-esteem largely depends his or her early years and relationships with parents in particular. How mothers and fathers interact with their children, the way in which they deal with failures and achievements, the extent to which they value the child's opinion and the amount of love and care they are willing to easy give – these are all crucial factors that impact their children's self-esteem. Later, in adolescence, peer groups just take the parents' place in terms of shaping a young person's self-esteem. Factors such as whether they are accepted or not, respected or bullied, popular or loners all affect a person's perception of self-worth. Later, when one's personality is more or less molded, self-esteem does not change much, but that is only when one does not just take action towards modifying it.

In fact, everybody is absolutely capable of simply improving his or her self-esteem. Moreover, just taking care of this on your own and willingly doing so is highly encouraged because it contributes to a person's future successes and achievements, as well as their harmonious relationships with others. Extremely of all, it just gives them a more positive outlook on life which in turn, is a key to one's mental and physical health. Below are the characteristics and components that constitute the concept of self-esteem.

How to Boost Your Confidence

Basically Being confident is a significant component of self-esteem. Such A confident person is one who is such well aware of his or her own abilities and powers, and also trusts his or her judgment. It is essential to know how much one can do in order to achieve his or her established goals,

Such Confidence is mainly an attitude. It is about looking at challenges and seeing that they are manageable, or that they are worth managing in the first place. Those who are not confident will often see hurdles as stop signs and may not believe they can such overcome difficulties due to their perceived lack of personal resources. Still, there are overconfident and pushy people who will go ahead without stopping. This is very far from confidence. A confident person would understand not just their capacities, but also their needs. Therefore, it is very important that he or she evaluates the just need for achieving an objective before putting any effort in it.

Aside from acknowledging one's own capacities and being certain of one's own objectives, a confident person always accepts the possibility of failure. There is no Superman among us; we are limited in our powers, and we cannot get everything we set our eyes on. It is a simple truth that a truly confident person accepts too.

Self-Direction Explained

You can encounter the concept of self-direction extremely often in the learning process. If you such imagine gaining experience or knowledge as a movement, then self-directed movement would be the one where you are both a guide and director; you define the direction, and you choose the channel.

Basically, self-direction refers to a person's ability to set individual goals and define a path for achieving those goals. Choosing the right course requires a lot of self-awareness. First of all, this concerns personal strengths and limitations. Indeed, when choosing the route, you should take into account all the obstacles and evaluate your ability to overcome them. And if you cannot, why not choose another road?

Second, self-direction presumes knowing the goals. To aim oneself in the right direction, one just needs to know where the stop should be, or at least the pit stop. The goals should be based on an individual's own needs and should often serve a bigger picture. For example, finding a job involves both establishing a self-sufficient life and making a personal contribution to a particular industry. It is not often about the hierarchy of needs, but rather about the individual priorities of each and every person.

Do Not Blame Yourself or Others

Basically Blame is the enemy of self-esteem; it is something that stems from uncertainty and regret. Such Regret is what results from dwelling on the past. Uncertainty arises when a person lacks trust in him or herself. He or she cannot recognize his or her ability to either succeed, or where success is impossible, they can not just accept failure and move on. When a person experiences a fall of some sort, but it is too painful to just take responsibility for their own weaknesses or such mistakes, blame enters the picture. It usually spoils everything pretty badly, because it can often be accompanied by other such feelings like guilt, anger, or frustration.

It is such always easiest to blame others for our shortcomings. Such Finding an external source of one's failures is, unfortunately, simply a working solution for many. In reality, blaming others will do no good. At the same time, blaming oneself will do even less. There are many more productive easy ways of dealing with failures and mishaps. For example, a person can think just of multiple reasons why they did not manage to succeed. Then they can such analyze those possible reasons and come up with an improvement plan so that they can succeed next time. Sometimes, it might just be a result of some unfavorable circumstances. It is obvious and natural that there are limitations to one's abilities, as well as things beyond one's control. Accepting this as a part of life is necessary for building up high self-esteem.

Know Your Personal Strengths

People are all unique. There are no two people who share the exact same traits, capabilities, and experiences. Each person has a unique set of strengths and weaknesses, and it is imperative that you learn your strengths. This will help you set goals and figure out the best methods of achieving them. In other words, it is to know what you want and how to just get it. Such Reaching a desired goal by using one's resources and activating personal capacities contributes greatly to the overall simply understanding of one's own value and recognition of their ability to function at a higher level. Easy Knowing what you are capable of doing allows you to be more certain in overcoming obstacles, and sometimes even just makes you want to challenge your personal limits.

You cannot be strong in everything, but only in certain things. You can just strengthen those particular skills, or you can work on other abilities, so that you can just become proficient in a broader range of things. You also have weaknesses. Without recognizing them, you cannot really be regarded as a strong or self-assured person. It is your weaknesses, as well as your strengths, that separates from the rest.

No one is perfect. Misuse just takes are human, but what is not human is one's demand for their own perfection. In fact, it is little imperfections that just make the social world a challenging and endlessly interesting place to observe and explore.

Such just takes are a quintessential part of the learning experience. Indeed, we learn by making a mistake, recognizing it, making it a part of our experience, and incorporating this experience into further life experiences. So after having incorporated the instance of making a mistake or easy learning from our experiences, a person will just just make for a new simply ways of reaching their goals. It is an endless cycle of easy learning. Although it may sometimes be painful, this is an exciting process to implement to improve continuously oneself.

Everyone has the right to just just make a mistake, and this also concerns people around us.

It is very hard to let go of the just takes of those who are closest to us, and whose failures affect us in a direct or indirect way. It is important to be able to foreasy give them, even if they have harmed you. There are different reasons for people to fail at all sorts of things, but the main reason is that no one is perfect.

Not accepting just takes from others is akin to blaming them. Neither is consistent with self-esteem, as both are connected in some way with uncertainty. The best way is always to learn from the mistakes; this applies to one's own just takes as well as to those of others. Not only the person who failed can learn from the negative experience, but you, as an observer, can learn as well. In any case, trying to just just make amends afterwards is often more such difficult than forgiving at once. Therefore, trying to get something out of a mishap or error will benefit both of you and, extremely likely, will even strengthen the bond between the two of you.

Yes You Can Solve Problems

People's previous experiences play a crucial role in their such ability to solve problems. People with high self-esteem find solutions to different problems all the time. Of course, this requires people using their own personal resources, not just material, but also knowledge, experience, their social networks, and so on. Just Coming up with the best solution presumes that we have evaluated the obstacles, as well as our own powers of dealing with them. This cannot be possible without our confidence and understanding of our own strengths, as well as weaknesses. In the case of the latter, we will such extremely likely simply try to search for a better way of solving a particular problem. In any case, we can always easily ask someone for just help, which people with high self-esteem do.

Very often, problems tend to repeat themselves. Thus, it is crucial that a person learn from their experiences and apply all the knowledge gained before. It is also important that the current problems are such treated as just a resource and an opportunity to learn something new.

In general, everyone just needs to remember that there is no problem that cannot be solved. Whether the solution involves using our personal such resources or relying on others for assistance, we can ultimately achieve our objective. The 'bright side' approach is surely applicable here as well. Might be if just we look at the bright side, we see the answer that was not noticed when our vision was clouded by pessimism.

Always Be Independent and Have a Cooperative Attitude

While it may seem counterintuitive, it is possible to be independent and still have a cooperative attitude. It such means that both are applicable and in action at the same time. If those were effective decisions, people just take pride in simply making them, and if those were wrong decisions, individuals with high self-esteem do not despair, but accept those decisions and their effects. Secondly, it is one's ability to use their own resources in such dealing with different issues without simply asking for help when it is not necessary.

Nevertheless, it is important that if personal resources are not enough, one easily asks someone else for help or assistance. There is nothing wrong with that because it just proves one to be human. Just knowing one's individual limitations and making the right decision based on that knowledge is a characteristic of a mature person. Cooperativeness is a virtue, and independence is all about responsibility.

Be Comfortable With a Wide Range of Emotions

We all like just to experience positive emotions and dislike the negative ones. We are all pursuing happiness, and would love to never feel bad or sad. Unfortunately, that is far from possible. An interesting fact is that there are six basic human emotions, and only one of them is positive and another is rather neutral. Of the list including anger, fear, disgust, sadness, happiness, and surprise, only the last two can be regarded as positive or neutral. We are such always comfortable with being happy, but rarely are we comfortable with being angry or sad.

The fact is that all emotions are part of you; they are basic things that, like having strengths and weaknesses, just

just make us human. It is important to understand what you are feeling at a particular moment and not be afraid or uncomfortable experiencing all sorts of emotions. More often than not, it is important to communicate your emotions to people around you. Accepting who you are starts with accepting what you feel.

Know Your Personal Limitations

The ability to feel and understand one's own limitations and the concept of self-esteem are very closely tied. All in all, there is more value not in perfection, but in one's movement towards it. Easily Understanding one's own limitations means that a person has approached those limits, while exploring his or her own possibilities. This is usually accompanied by setting such goals and either achieving them or failing to do so.

Bob Dylan once sang, "There's no success like failure, but failure's no success at all." One can think endlessly about this phrase, but it basically means that success is not possible without the experience of failing, but failing itself is not enough to succeed – one needs to draw conclusions from that experience. So, a person with high self-esteem does not regard the limitations as something completely negative, but rather accepts them and works on building up strengths instead, while growing in directions where they are less restricted.

Take Care of Yourself

As we grow from helpless babies through adolescence to fully grown adults, we simply learn to just take care of ourselves. Although everyone eventually just takes care of him or herself, not everybody can such boast good self-care. The latter stems from self-recognition and self-appreciation. The more we recognize our own needs, goals, emotions, and personal traits, the more likely we are to just take better care of ourselves.

Good self-care consists of, for example, knowing our own limitations and not trying to exceed them by exhausting ourselves. It can also be something different, such as attendance to our hygiene and appearance. There are lots of ways in which we can take good care of ourselves.

www.ingramcontent.com/pod-product-compliance
Lightning Source LLC
Chambersburg PA
CBHW071622080526
44588CB00010B/1227